D1363730

Christmas

Dennis Brindell Fradin

—*Best Holiday Books*—

Enslow Publishers, Inc.

40 Industrial Road   PO Box 38
Box 398   Aldershot
Berkeley Heights, NJ 07922   Hants GU12 6BP
USA   UK

http://www.enslow.com

> *For my dear friends Bill, Joan, Valerie, Mike, and Peter Schmitt*

Library of Congress Cataloging-in-Publication Data
Fradin, Dennis B.
    Christmas / by Dennis Brindell Fradin.
       p.   cm. — (Best holiday books)
    Summary: Describes the history behind Christmas and the various ways it is celebrated.
     ISBN 0-89490-258-X
    1. Christmas—Juvenile literature. [1. Christmas.] I. Title.
  II. Series: Fradin, Dennis B. Best holiday books.
  GT4985.5.F73 1990
  394.2'68282—dc20   89-25634
                                       CIP
                                       AC

Printed in the United States of America

10 9 8 7

Illustration Credits:
Tom Dunnington: pp. 17, 19; Hallmark Historical Collection, Hallmark Cards, Inc.: pp. 25, 33, 36, 37; Photo by Jerry Hennen: p. 21; Historical Pictures Service, Chicago: pp. 12, 14; John F. Kennedy Library: p. 41; Library of Congress: pp. 6, 7, 10, 32, 34; Rudolph and Rudolph the Red-Nosed Reindeer are the registered trademarks of the Robert L. May Co., Novato, California: p. 40; Norma Morrison: p. 4; National Park Service: p. 28; Religious News Service: p. 24; The Salvation Army Metropolitan Division, Chicago: p. 44

Cover Illustration by Charlott Nathan

Contents

People and even cats are curious about the presents under the Christmas tree.

A Merry Christmas to All!

Each December 25, millions of people celebrate Christmas. This holiday honors the birth of Jesus Christ, who founded the Christian religion about 2,000 years ago. The name "Christ" is part of the word Christmas.

Christmas customs vary from place to place. In the United States, many families set up "Christmas trees" before December 25. They hang lights and candy canes on the trees. Some families hang Christmas wreaths on their doors. And some set up an outdoor "Nativity scene" showing the newborn Jesus Christ.

As Christmas approaches, millions of

Saint Nicholas, or Santa Claus as he is often called, is often portrayed as jolly and kind.

A family of 100 years ago enjoying their Christmas tree

children write to a magical man named Santa Claus who is said to live at the North Pole. They hope that Santa will bring them gifts on Christmas Eve (the night before Christmas). Schoolchildren draw pictures of Santa and his reindeer as art projects. And many schools have a winter assembly that may include a Christmas play and the singing of Christmas carols (songs).

Finally, the sun rises on December 25, Christmas morning. Millions of children find gifts waiting for them under their Christmas trees. The gifts may say "FROM SANTA CLAUS" or "FROM MOM AND DAD." Many adults have Christmas gifts waiting for them, too. These may be drawings or crafts made by their children in school.

Because Christmas honors the founder of Christianity, many families pray at church or at home on December 25. And millions of families have a big Christmas dinner much like the Thanksgiving feasts in November.

The Birth and Life of Jesus Christ

We know little about Jesus Christ's birth. Most of what we do know comes from the books of Saint Matthew and Saint Luke. Both books are in the part of the Bible called the New Testament.

Saint Luke wrote that a couple named Mary and Joseph lived in Nazareth (in modern Israel). One day the angel Gabriel told Mary that she was going to have a special baby. This baby, who was to be named Jesus, would be the son of God.

Near the time the baby was due, Mary and Joseph had to visit Bethlehem, almost 100 miles

Jesus Christ, the founder of Christianity, with his mother, the Virgin Mary

from Nazareth, to pay taxes. When the couple reached Bethlehem, there was no room for them at the inn. Joseph fixed up a stable as a shelter where Mary could have her baby.

Mary had her baby in the stable and named him Jesus as Gabriel had said. She and Joseph used a manger (a feed box for animals) as Jesus's cradle. According to Saint Luke, an angel told shepherds near Bethlehem about Jesus's birth. The shepherds came to the stable to see Jesus. The shepherds then spread the good news about the birth of the son of God.

According to Saint Matthew, a magic star appeared in the sky after Jesus's birth. Wise men from the east followed the star until they reached the stable in Bethlehem. The wise men gave Jesus gold and other gifts.

As an adult, Jesus became a preacher. He taught that people should be kind to each other. Luke wrote that Jesus said, "As ye would that men should do to you, do ye also to them likewise." This is the famous

The wise men coming to see Jesus

Golden Rule. It means that we should treat people the way we want to be treated. Jesus also taught that it is better to make peace than win wars. And he had a special place in his heart for poor and sick people.

To help people and to prove who he was, Jesus performed miracles. He healed blind and sick people. Once he brought a dead man named Lazarus back to life. Many people who believed that Jesus was God's son became his followers. Twelve close followers, called the 12 apostles, helped spread Jesus's teachings.

Meanwhile, Jesus was making enemies. Some people didn't believe he was God's son. Some of the Romans who ruled Jesus's homeland of Palestine feared that he would lead a revolt against them. Pontius Pilate, the Roman governor of Palestine, sentenced Jesus to die on the cross. After this sentence was carried out, Jesus's body was placed in a tomb. But the New Testament relates that Jesus came back to life and met with his friends for several weeks. Then

Many early Christians were mistreated. These Christians have been dis-
covered in their hiding place by Roman soldiers.

he went to heaven to be with God, his father.

The religion Jesus founded became known as Christianity. Although the early Christians were mistreated, the religion kept spreading. Today, Christianity is the world's largest religion with over 1 1/2 billion followers.

Christmas Becomes a Holiday

Many nations including the United States count time in relation to Jesus's birth. The years before Jesus's birth belong to the B.C. (standing for "Before Christ") period. The years after Jesus's birth belong to the A.D. (standing for *Anno Domini*, which means "in the Year of the Lord") period. Something that happened in 150 B.C. took place 150 years before Christ's birth. Something that happened in 300 A.D. occurred 300 years after Christ's birth.

We don't know if Jesus's birthday was honored during Christianity's first 300 years. But a very old calendar tells us that it was honored by 336 A.D. It was held on December 25, the same as today.

Actually, we don't know the real month and day of Jesus's birth. Perhaps it was December 25. But it could have been June 25 or any other day of the year. Why was December 25 chosen? To answer that, it helps to know a little about early Christianity.

Early Christian priests could not get

Long ago, people feared the long nights that came with winter. They wondered if longer days would ever come again.

everyone to give up their old gods and holidays. They called people who worshiped various old gods, pagans. Even many Christians celebrated both Christian and pagan holidays. The priests thought of a way to make people forget the old pagan holidays. They placed Christian holidays on the same days of the year as the old pagan holidays. They wanted the Christian holidays to slowly replace the pagan ones. That was exactly what happened.

Halloween was placed on October 31 because of an old pagan holiday that was held then. Valentine's Day (February 14) may have replaced a pagan holiday that came on February 15. Christmas seems to have been placed on December 25 to replace pagan winter rites that were held around that time.

Winter starts for the earth's northern half on December 21 or 22. That first day of winter has the longest night of any day of the year. Ancient people probably feared that the nights might keep getting longer until the sun didn't rise at all! But soon after December 21 or 22, they could see that the days were getting longer.

Many ancient people held rites in late December to thank their gods for making the days longer. For example, the Persians held a

When the days began getting longer in late December, many ancient people held rites to thank their gods for saving them from the darkness.

festival honoring Mithras, their god of light. Christmas was probably placed in late December in the hope that it would replace these pagan winter rites. The plan worked. The pagan winter holidays were slowly forgotten as Christmas grew in importance.

At first Christmas was much different than it is now. There was no Santa Claus tradition as yet. Some people gave Christmas gifts, but priests didn't like this. Gift giving had been part of the pagan winter rites. Church leaders wanted Christmas to be a purely religious holiday.

At first Christmas was mainly a time for prayer. By the fifth century after the birth of Christ, the Pope in Rome was saying three special ceremonies called masses on Christmas. The first mass was at midnight of Christmas Eve. The second was at sunrise of December 25. The third mass came later on that Christmas Day. The word Christmas means "Christ's mass."

Many Christians go to church on Christmas Eve and Christmas Day.

Leaders sometimes chose Christmas for important acts. Charlemagne was crowned emperor by Pope Leo III on Christmas Day of 800 A.D. Charlemagne was the king of most of Europe. It was also said that King Arthur obtained his magic sword, Excalibur, on Christmas Day long ago.

Enter Saint Nicholas

Christian priests wanted Christmas to be a purely religious day. But during Europe's Middle Ages (about 400 A.D.—about 1500 A.D.) Christmas slowly became a day for fun, too. Gift giving became as popular as it had been during the pagan winter rites. The giving of gifts became linked to Saint Nicholas in many people's minds.

Nicholas was a Christian bishop who lived around 300 A.D. He was known as a friend to children, sailors, and the poor. After Nicholas's death he was named a saint—a very holy person. His fame kept growing. By the late 1400s only Jesus and his

Long ago, Saint Nicholas was thought to travel on a horse. His basket contains gifts for good children.

In more recent times, Saint Nicholas has been pictured as traveling in a sleigh pulled by reindeer.

mother Mary were more popular among Christians than Saint Nicholas. Thousands of boys were named for him. England alone had about 400 churches named for him.

December 6, the day of Nicholas's death, became a holiday in much of Europe. Many children believed that Nicholas rode his horse across the sky on the night of December 5. He was said to leave gifts for good children. On the morning of December 6 (Saint Nicholas Day), many children found sweets and other treats in the shoes they had left by their fireplaces.

During the 1500s a new form of Christianity was born. It was called Protestantism. Protestant leaders felt that Nicholas and other saints received too much attention. People in some places then moved Saint Nicholas's visit 19 days later to Christmas Eve. By then gift giving had become an established part of Christmas. People knew that religious leaders would complain less if the Saint Nicholas gift-giving customs were mixed with Christmas.

Christmas Comes to America

Europeans began settling what is now the United States in the early 1600s. America's early colonists included English, German, and Dutch people. These people brought their Christmas customs to America.

English people brought the custom of hanging up plants called holly and mistletoe at Christmas. To this day, many Americans hang Christmas wreaths made from holly on their doors. And some people still follow the English custom that a man who sees a woman standing under mistletoe can kiss her.

By the late 1500s, people in Germany had set

A national Christmas tree is set up every year in Washington, D.C.

up "Christmas trees" in their homes. German people who came to America brought this custom with them.

As for the Santa Claus tradition, that was brought to America by the Dutch (people of the Netherlands). Dutch children referred to Saint Nicholas as Sinterklass. They believed that he visited their homes on the night of December 5. Other children in America adopted the Sinterklass belief. They said his name so fast that it became Santa Claus. Over time his visit was moved from the night of December 5 to Christmas Eve for most American children.

Christmas Becomes VERY Popular

As of the year 1800, Christmas wasn't nearly as popular as it is now in the United States. Some Americans hadn't even heard of Santa Claus. But by the late 1800s, Christmas and Santa Claus were very popular. What caused this change?

An author and an artist helped spread Santa's fame. Near Christmas of 1823, a poem by Clement Clarke Moore of New York City appeared in a newspaper. It began with the lines:

'Twas the night before Christmas,
when all through the house

Not a creature was stirring,
    not even a mouse;
The stockings were hung
    by the chimney with care,
In hopes that Saint Nicholas
    soon would be there.

The poem tells how a father sees Santa Claus one Christmas Eve. Santa in this poem is a "jolly old elf" with a beard "white as the snow," a "little round belly," and a nose "like a cherry." Millions of Americans read this poem. It helped create a picture of Santa that has lasted to this day.

Between 1863 and 1886 the artist Thomas Nast drew many pictures of Santa for *Harper's Weekly* magazine. Nast drew Santa much as Clement Clarke Moore had described him, but added a few details. One was that Santa lived at the North Pole. By the late 1800s Nast's drawings, Moore's poems, and other stories and poems had made Santa famous across America.

Clement Clarke Moore, the author of "The Night Before Christmas"

Christmas carols also helped popularize Christmas during the 1800s. At Christmastime of 1818 a priest in Oberndorf, Austria, named Joseph Mohr found that the church organ didn't work. Mice had eaten away at it. Mohr decided to write a Christmas song for voice and guitar. He wrote the words to "Silent Night" on Christmas Eve of 1818. That same night Franz Gruber, the church organist, wrote the melody

Children singing Christmas carols

Santa is reading letters from naughty and good children in this Thomas Nast drawing.

for "Silent Night." This great carol was first sung at the Oberndorf church later on that Christmas Eve of 1818. It became very popular in the United States and in many other parts of the world.

Other Christmas carols that were written during the 1800s included "It Came Upon a Midnight Clear," "I Heard the Bells on Christmas Day," and "O Little Town of Bethlehem." Some very old Christmas carols were first printed in books during the 1800s. For example, the old French carol "The First Noel" first appeared in a book in 1833. The version of the old English carol "The Twelve Days of Christmas" that is most popular today was first published in 1842.

Many people couldn't afford to give gifts and eat a Christmas feast. But everyone could sing Christmas carols! In this way carols helped bring Christmas to more people than ever before during the 1800s.

This Christmas card was made by Louis Prang in 1886.

The first Christmas card by John Calcott Horsley

Christmas cards also involved more people in the holiday. In 1843 an English children's book publisher named Henry Cole asked an artist friend to make a card for Christmas. The friend, John Calcott Horsley, designed the first professional Christmas card. About 1,000 copies of it were printed. In 1875 Louis Prang of Boston printed some of the first Christmas cards in the United States. Cards were an easy, cheap way to send Christmas wishes. Since the late 1800s they have helped spread Christmas cheer to millions of people.

Christmas in Our Time

Many people still go to church on Christmas. In general, though, Americans focus less on the religious side of Christmas than they once did. As a result, most modern Christmas songs, stories, and films are not religious.

In 1942 Bing Crosby sang "White Christmas" by Irving Berlin in the film *Holiday Inn.* "White Christmas," which expresses the hope that it will snow for Christmas, became one of the most popular songs ever recorded. In 1949 Gene Autry recorded "Rudolph the Red-Nosed Reindeer®" by Johnny Marks. This song, which tells the story of a red-nosed reindeer who led Santa's sleigh one foggy Christmas Eve, also became a great hit.

Each year many Christmas films can be seen on TV and in theaters. Several films have been made of *A Christmas Carol* by Charles Dickens. This famous story is about a selfish man named

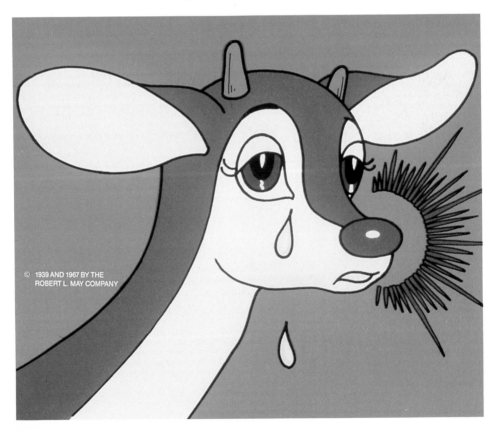

Rudolph the Red-Nosed Reindeer®

President John F. Kennedy taking his children's stockings down from the chimney on Christmas morning, 1962

Scrooge who learns the meaning of Christmas. *Miracle on 34th Street*, a movie about a man who claims he is the real Santa Claus, also appears often on TV. A more recent film, *A Christmas Story*, shows how one American family spent the holiday in the mid-1900s.

Not everyone is happy with the way Christmas is celebrated in our time. Many people think that Christmas has become too "commercial." This means that they think gift giving and Christmas decorations have become too important.

It is certainly true that Christmas decorations and gifts have become very important. Ads for Christmas gifts start appearing around October. Millions of Americans now decorate not just the inside but the outside of their homes for Christmas. In some neighborhoods the outside of nearly every building is decorated with colored lights and Santa Claus statues.

Yet the love and kindness that make up the

"Christmas spirit" are very much alive. Millions of families hold Christmas parties that are much like those their great-grandparents enjoyed. Each branch of the family may bring food to the gathering. The family shares a great feast. They may exchange gifts, sing Christmas carols, and share memories of past Christmases. Many people's happiest memories are of their family Christmas parties.

The Christmas season is also a traditional time to remember needy people. Each Christmas, many children go to hospitals to sing carols for the patients. Adults and children give money to help buy Christmas gifts and food for the poor. And some people help fix Christmas dinners for the poor at community centers. The founder of Christianity would have liked these acts of kindness. But wouldn't he have wanted the "Christmas spirit" to last all year long?

This girl is helping to raise money for poor people at Christmastime.

Glossary

A.D.—this refers to the years after the birth of Jesus
Christ

apostles—followers who help spread a
person's teachings

B.C.—this refers to the years before Jesus
Christ was born

bishop—a high-ranking church official

century—a period of 100 years

Christianity—the religion that Jesus Christ
founded about 2,000 years ago

Christmas carols—Christmas songs

Christmas Eve—the night before Christmas

emperor—king

million—a thousand thousand (1,000,000)

miracle—an amazing event that is thought to show God's will

Nativity scene—a decoration that shows the birth of Jesus Christ

Noel—the French word for "Christmas"

pagans—people who believe in more than one god

saint—a very holy person

shepherds—people who take care of sheep

wreath—a round decoration often made of plants